Expectant Mothers

Fitness Tracker

Fitness Journal Happy Planner

Activinotes

Activinotes

DAILY JOURNALS, PLANNERS, NOTEBOOKS AND OTHER BLANK BOOKS

DAILY FOOD INTAKE & FITNESS ROUTINE

BREAKFAST

TIME:

DESCRIPTION:

PROTEIN	CARBS	FATS	FRUITS / VEGGIES	CALORIES

SNACK

TIME:

DESCRIPTION:

PROTEIN	CARBS	FATS	FRUITS / VEGGIES	CALORIES

LUNCH

TIME:

DESCRIPTION:

PROTEIN	CARBS	FATS	FRUITS / VEGGIES	CALORIES

SNACK

DESCRIPTION:

PROTEIN	CARBS	FATS	FRUITS / VEGGIES	CALORIES

DINNER

DESCRIPTION:

PROTEIN	CARBS	FATS	FRUITS / VEGGIES	CALORIES

TODAYS WORKOUT

EXERCISE	SETS	REPS	WEIGHT	REST	NOTE

DAILY FOOD INTAKE & FITNESS ROUTINE

BREAKFAST

TIME:

DESCRIPTION:

PROTEIN	CARBS	FATS	FRUITS / VEGGIES	CALORIES

SNACK

TIME:

DESCRIPTION:

PROTEIN	CARBS	FATS	FRUITS / VEGGIES	CALORIES

LUNCH

TIME:

DESCRIPTION:

PROTEIN	CARBS	FATS	FRUITS / VEGGIES	CALORIES

SNACK

DESCRIPTION:

PROTEIN	CARBS	FATS	FRUITS / VEGGIES	CALORIES

DINNER

TIME:

DESCRIPTION:

PROTEIN	CARBS	FATS	FRUITS / VEGGIES	CALORIES

TODAYS WORKOUT

TIME:

EXERCISE	SETS	REPS	WEIGHT	REST	NOTE

DAILY FOOD INTAKE & FITNESS ROUTINE

BREAKFAST

TIME:

DESCRIPTION:

PROTEIN	CARBS	FATS	FRUITS / VEGGIES	CALORIES

SNACK

TIME:

DESCRIPTION:

PROTEIN	CARBS	FATS	FRUITS / VEGGIES	CALORIES

LUNCH

TIME:

DESCRIPTION:

PROTEIN	CARBS	FATS	FRUITS / VEGGIES	CALORIES

SNACK

DESCRIPTION:

PROTEIN	CARBS	FATS	FRUITS / VEGGIES	CALORIES

DINNER

TIME:

DESCRIPTION:

PROTEIN	CARBS	FATS	FRUITS / VEGGIES	CALORIES

TODAYS WORKOUT

TIME:

EXERCISE	SETS	REPS	WEIGHT	REST	NOTE

DAILY FOOD INTAKE & FITNESS ROUTINE

BREAKFAST

TIME:

DESCRIPTION:

PROTEIN	CARBS	FATS	FRUITS / VEGGIES	CALORIES

SNACK

TIME:

DESCRIPTION:

PROTEIN	CARBS	FATS	FRUITS / VEGGIES	CALORIES

LUNCH

TIME:

DESCRIPTION:

PROTEIN	CARBS	FATS	FRUITS / VEGGIES	CALORIES

SNACK

DESCRIPTION:

PROTEIN	CARBS	FATS	FRUITS / VEGGIES	CALORIES

DINNER

TIME:

DESCRIPTION:

PROTEIN	CARBS	FATS	FRUITS / VEGGIES	CALORIES

TODAYS WORKOUT

TIME:

EXERCISE	SETS	REPS	WEIGHT	REST	NOTE

DAILY FOOD INTAKE & FITNESS ROUTINE

BREAKFAST

TIME:

DESCRIPTION:

PROTEIN	CARBS	FATS	FRUITS / VEGGIES	CALORIES

SNACK

TIME:

DESCRIPTION:

PROTEIN	CARBS	FATS	FRUITS / VEGGIES	CALORIES

LUNCH

TIME:

DESCRIPTION:

PROTEIN	CARBS	FATS	FRUITS / VEGGIES	CALORIES

SNACK

DESCRIPTION:

PROTEIN	CARBS	FATS	FRUITS / VEGGIES	CALORIES

DINNER

TIME:

DESCRIPTION:

PROTEIN	CARBS	FATS	FRUITS / VEGGIES	CALORIES

TODAYS WORKOUT

TIME:

EXERCISE	SETS	REPS	WEIGHT	REST	NOTE

DAILY FOOD INTAKE & FITNESS ROUTINE

BREAKFAST

TIME:

DESCRIPTION:

PROTEIN	CARBS	FATS	FRUITS / VEGGIES	CALORIES

SNACK

TIME:

DESCRIPTION:

PROTEIN	CARBS	FATS	FRUITS / VEGGIES	CALORIES

LUNCH

TIME:

DESCRIPTION:

PROTEIN	CARBS	FATS	FRUITS / VEGGIES	CALORIES

SNACK

DESCRIPTION:

PROTEIN	CARBS	FATS	FRUITS / VEGGIES	CALORIES

DINNER

TIME:

DESCRIPTION:

PROTEIN	CARBS	FATS	FRUITS / VEGGIES	CALORIES

TODAYS WORKOUT

TIME:

EXERCISE	SETS	REPS	WEIGHT	REST	NOTE

DAILY FOOD INTAKE & FITNESS ROUTINE

BREAKFAST

TIME:

DESCRIPTION:

PROTEIN	CARBS	FATS	FRUITS / VEGGIES	CALORIES

SNACK

TIME:

DESCRIPTION:

PROTEIN	CARBS	FATS	FRUITS / VEGGIES	CALORIES

LUNCH

TIME:

DESCRIPTION:

PROTEIN	CARBS	FATS	FRUITS / VEGGIES	CALORIES

SNACK

DESCRIPTION:

PROTEIN	CARBS	FATS	FRUITS / VEGGIES	CALORIES

DINNER

TIME:

DESCRIPTION:

PROTEIN	CARBS	FATS	FRUITS / VEGGIES	CALORIES

TODAYS WORKOUT

TIME:

EXERCISE	SETS	REPS	WEIGHT	REST	NOTE

DAILY FOOD INTAKE & FITNESS ROUTINE

BREAKFAST

TIME:

DESCRIPTION:

PROTEIN	CARBS	FATS	FRUITS / VEGGIES	CALORIES

SNACK

TIME:

DESCRIPTION:

PROTEIN	CARBS	FATS	FRUITS / VEGGIES	CALORIES

LUNCH

TIME:

DESCRIPTION:

PROTEIN	CARBS	FATS	FRUITS / VEGGIES	CALORIES

SNACK

DESCRIPTION:

PROTEIN	CARBS	FATS	FRUITS / VEGGIES	CALORIES

DINNER

TIME:

DESCRIPTION:

PROTEIN	CARBS	FATS	FRUITS / VEGGIES	CALORIES

TODAYS WORKOUT

TIME:

EXERCISE	SETS	REPS	WEIGHT	REST	NOTE

DAILY FOOD INTAKE & FITNESS ROUTINE

BREAKFAST

TIME:

DESCRIPTION:

PROTEIN	CARBS	FATS	FRUITS / VEGGIES	CALORIES

SNACK

TIME:

DESCRIPTION:

PROTEIN	CARBS	FATS	FRUITS / VEGGIES	CALORIES

LUNCH

TIME:

DESCRIPTION:

PROTEIN	CARBS	FATS	FRUITS / VEGGIES	CALORIES

SNACK

TIME:

DESCRIPTION:

_____

_____

_____

PROTEIN	CARBS	FATS	FRUITS / VEGGIES	CALORIES

DINNER

TIME:

DESCRIPTION:

_____

_____

_____

_____

_____

PROTEIN	CARBS	FATS	FRUITS / VEGGIES	CALORIES

TODAYS WORKOUT

TIME:

EXERCISE	SETS	REPS	WEIGHT	REST	NOTE

DAILY FOOD INTAKE & FITNESS ROUTINE

BREAKFAST

TIME:

DESCRIPTION:

PROTEIN	CARBS	FATS	FRUITS / VEGGIES	CALORIES

SNACK

TIME:

DESCRIPTION:

PROTEIN	CARBS	FATS	FRUITS / VEGGIES	CALORIES

LUNCH

TIME:

DESCRIPTION:

PROTEIN	CARBS	FATS	FRUITS / VEGGIES	CALORIES

SNACK

DESCRIPTION:

PROTEIN	CARBS	FATS	FRUITS / VEGGIES	CALORIES

DINNER

TIME:

DESCRIPTION:

PROTEIN	CARBS	FATS	FRUITS / VEGGIES	CALORIES

TODAYS WORKOUT

TIME:

EXERCISE	SETS	REPS	WEIGHT	REST	NOTE

DAILY FOOD INTAKE & FITNESS ROUTINE

BREAKFAST

TIME:

DESCRIPTION:

PROTEIN	CARBS	FATS	FRUITS / VEGGIES	CALORIES

SNACK

TIME:

DESCRIPTION:

PROTEIN	CARBS	FATS	FRUITS / VEGGIES	CALORIES

LUNCH

TIME:

DESCRIPTION:

PROTEIN	CARBS	FATS	FRUITS / VEGGIES	CALORIES

SNACK

DESCRIPTION:

PROTEIN	CARBS	FATS	FRUITS / VEGGIES	CALORIES

DINNER

TIME:

DESCRIPTION:

PROTEIN	CARBS	FATS	FRUITS / VEGGIES	CALORIES

TODAYS WORKOUT

TIME:

EXERCISE	SETS	REPS	WEIGHT	REST	NOTE

DAILY FOOD INTAKE & FITNESS ROUTINE

BREAKFAST

TIME:

DESCRIPTION:

PROTEIN	CARBS	FATS	FRUITS / VEGGIES	CALORIES

SNACK

TIME:

DESCRIPTION:

PROTEIN	CARBS	FATS	FRUITS / VEGGIES	CALORIES

LUNCH

TIME:

DESCRIPTION:

PROTEIN	CARBS	FATS	FRUITS / VEGGIES	CALORIES

SNACK

DESCRIPTION:

PROTEIN	CARBS	FATS	FRUITS / VEGGIES	CALORIES

DINNER

TIME:

DESCRIPTION:

PROTEIN	CARBS	FATS	FRUITS / VEGGIES	CALORIES

TODAYS WORKOUT

TIME:

EXERCISE	SETS	REPS	WEIGHT	REST	NOTE

DAILY FOOD INTAKE & FITNESS ROUTINE

BREAKFAST

TIME:

DESCRIPTION:

PROTEIN	CARBS	FATS	FRUITS / VEGGIES	CALORIES

SNACK

TIME:

DESCRIPTION:

PROTEIN	CARBS	FATS	FRUITS / VEGGIES	CALORIES

LUNCH

TIME:

DESCRIPTION:

PROTEIN	CARBS	FATS	FRUITS / VEGGIES	CALORIES

SNACK

TIME:

DESCRIPTION:

_____

_____

_____

PROTEIN	CARBS	FATS	FRUITS / VEGGIES	CALORIES

DINNER

TIME:

DESCRIPTION:

_____

_____

_____

_____

_____

PROTEIN	CARBS	FATS	FRUITS / VEGGIES	CALORIES

TODAYS WORKOUT

TIME:

EXERCISE	SETS	REPS	WEIGHT	REST	NOTE

DAILY FOOD INTAKE & FITNESS ROUTINE

BREAKFAST

TIME:

DESCRIPTION:

PROTEIN	CARBS	FATS	FRUITS / VEGGIES	CALORIES

SNACK

TIME:

DESCRIPTION:

PROTEIN	CARBS	FATS	FRUITS / VEGGIES	CALORIES

LUNCH

TIME:

DESCRIPTION:

PROTEIN	CARBS	FATS	FRUITS / VEGGIES	CALORIES

SNACK

TIME:

DESCRIPTION:

PROTEIN	CARBS	FATS	FRUITS / VEGGIES	CALORIES

DINNER

TIME:

DESCRIPTION:

PROTEIN	CARBS	FATS	FRUITS / VEGGIES	CALORIES

TODAYS WORKOUT

TIME:

EXERCISE	SETS	REPS	WEIGHT	REST	NOTE

DAILY FOOD INTAKE & FITNESS ROUTINE

BREAKFAST

TIME:

DESCRIPTION:

PROTEIN	CARBS	FATS	FRUITS / VEGGIES	CALORIES

SNACK

TIME:

DESCRIPTION:

PROTEIN	CARBS	FATS	FRUITS / VEGGIES	CALORIES

LUNCH

TIME:

DESCRIPTION:

PROTEIN	CARBS	FATS	FRUITS / VEGGIES	CALORIES

SNACK

DESCRIPTION:

_____

_____

_____

PROTEIN	CARBS	FATS	FRUITS / VEGGIES	CALORIES

DINNER

TIME:

DESCRIPTION:

_____

_____

_____

_____

_____

PROTEIN	CARBS	FATS	FRUITS / VEGGIES	CALORIES

TODAYS WORKOUT

TIME:

EXERCISE	SETS	REPS	WEIGHT	REST	NOTE

DAILY FOOD INTAKE & FITNESS ROUTINE

BREAKFAST

TIME:

DESCRIPTION:

PROTEIN	CARBS	FATS	FRUITS / VEGGIES	CALORIES

SNACK

TIME:

DESCRIPTION:

PROTEIN	CARBS	FATS	FRUITS / VEGGIES	CALORIES

LUNCH

TIME:

DESCRIPTION:

PROTEIN	CARBS	FATS	FRUITS / VEGGIES	CALORIES

SNACK

DESCRIPTION:

PROTEIN	CARBS	FATS	FRUITS / VEGGIES	CALORIES

DINNER

TIME:

DESCRIPTION:

PROTEIN	CARBS	FATS	FRUITS / VEGGIES	CALORIES

TODAYS WORKOUT

TIME:

EXERCISE	SETS	REPS	WEIGHT	REST	NOTE

DAILY FOOD INTAKE & FITNESS ROUTINE

BREAKFAST

TIME:

DESCRIPTION:

PROTEIN	CARBS	FATS	FRUITS / VEGGIES	CALORIES

SNACK

TIME:

DESCRIPTION:

PROTEIN	CARBS	FATS	FRUITS / VEGGIES	CALORIES

LUNCH

TIME:

DESCRIPTION:

PROTEIN	CARBS	FATS	FRUITS / VEGGIES	CALORIES

SNACK

TIME:

DESCRIPTION:

_____

_____

_____

PROTEIN	CARBS	FATS	FRUITS / VEGGIES	CALORIES

DINNER

TIME:

DESCRIPTION:

_____

_____

_____

_____

_____

PROTEIN	CARBS	FATS	FRUITS / VEGGIES	CALORIES

TODAYS WORKOUT

TIME:

EXERCISE	SETS	REPS	WEIGHT	REST	NOTE

DAILY FOOD INTAKE & FITNESS ROUTINE

BREAKFAST

TIME:

DESCRIPTION:

PROTEIN	CARBS	FATS	FRUITS / VEGGIES	CALORIES

SNACK

TIME:

DESCRIPTION:

PROTEIN	CARBS	FATS	FRUITS / VEGGIES	CALORIES

LUNCH

TIME:

DESCRIPTION:

PROTEIN	CARBS	FATS	FRUITS / VEGGIES	CALORIES

SNACK

DESCRIPTION:

PROTEIN	CARBS	FATS	FRUITS / VEGGIES	CALORIES

DINNER

TIME:

DESCRIPTION:

PROTEIN	CARBS	FATS	FRUITS / VEGGIES	CALORIES

TODAYS WORKOUT

TIME:

EXERCISE	SETS	REPS	WEIGHT	REST	NOTE

DAILY FOOD INTAKE & FITNESS ROUTINE

BREAKFAST

TIME:

DESCRIPTION:

_____
_____
_____
_____
_____

PROTEIN	CARBS	FATS	FRUITS / VEGGIES	CALORIES

SNACK

TIME:

DESCRIPTION:

_____
_____
_____

PROTEIN	CARBS	FATS	FRUITS / VEGGIES	CALORIES

LUNCH

TIME:

DESCRIPTION:

_____
_____
_____
_____
_____

PROTEIN	CARBS	FATS	FRUITS / VEGGIES	CALORIES

SNACK

DESCRIPTION:

PROTEIN	CARBS	FATS	FRUITS / VEGGIES	CALORIES

DINNER

TIME:

DESCRIPTION:

PROTEIN	CARBS	FATS	FRUITS / VEGGIES	CALORIES

TODAYS WORKOUT

TIME:

EXERCISE	SETS	REPS	WEIGHT	REST	NOTE

DAILY FOOD INTAKE & FITNESS ROUTINE

BREAKFAST

TIME:

DESCRIPTION:

PROTEIN	CARBS	FATS	FRUITS / VEGGIES	CALORIES

SNACK

TIME:

DESCRIPTION:

PROTEIN	CARBS	FATS	FRUITS / VEGGIES	CALORIES

LUNCH

TIME:

DESCRIPTION:

PROTEIN	CARBS	FATS	FRUITS / VEGGIES	CALORIES

SNACK

DESCRIPTION:

PROTEIN	CARBS	FATS	FRUITS / VEGGIES	CALORIES

DINNER

DESCRIPTION:

PROTEIN	CARBS	FATS	FRUITS / VEGGIES	CALORIES

TODAYS WORKOUT

EXERCISE	SETS	REPS	WEIGHT	REST	NOTE

DAILY FOOD INTAKE & FITNESS ROUTINE

BREAKFAST

TIME:

DESCRIPTION:

PROTEIN	CARBS	FATS	FRUITS / VEGGIES	CALORIES

SNACK

TIME:

DESCRIPTION:

PROTEIN	CARBS	FATS	FRUITS / VEGGIES	CALORIES

LUNCH

TIME:

DESCRIPTION:

PROTEIN	CARBS	FATS	FRUITS / VEGGIES	CALORIES

SNACK

DESCRIPTION: _____

_____

_____

PROTEIN	CARBS	FATS	FRUITS / VEGGIES	CALORIES

DINNER

TIME:

DESCRIPTION: _____

_____

_____

_____

_____

PROTEIN	CARBS	FATS	FRUITS / VEGGIES	CALORIES

TODAYS WORKOUT

TIME:

EXERCISE	SETS	REPS	WEIGHT	REST	NOTE

DAILY FOOD INTAKE & FITNESS ROUTINE

BREAKFAST

TIME:

DESCRIPTION:

PROTEIN	CARBS	FATS	FRUITS / VEGGIES	CALORIES

SNACK

TIME:

DESCRIPTION:

PROTEIN	CARBS	FATS	FRUITS / VEGGIES	CALORIES

LUNCH

TIME:

DESCRIPTION:

PROTEIN	CARBS	FATS	FRUITS / VEGGIES	CALORIES

SNACK

DESCRIPTION:

PROTEIN	CARBS	FATS	FRUITS / VEGGIES	CALORIES

DINNER

TIME:

DESCRIPTION:

PROTEIN	CARBS	FATS	FRUITS / VEGGIES	CALORIES

TODAYS WORKOUT

TIME:

EXERCISE	SETS	REPS	WEIGHT	REST	NOTE

DAILY FOOD INTAKE & FITNESS ROUTINE

BREAKFAST

TIME:

DESCRIPTION:

PROTEIN	CARBS	FATS	FRUITS / VEGGIES	CALORIES

SNACK

TIME:

DESCRIPTION:

PROTEIN	CARBS	FATS	FRUITS / VEGGIES	CALORIES

LUNCH

TIME:

DESCRIPTION:

PROTEIN	CARBS	FATS	FRUITS / VEGGIES	CALORIES

SNACK

DESCRIPTION:

PROTEIN	CARBS	FATS	FRUITS / VEGGIES	CALORIES

DINNER

TIME:

DESCRIPTION:

PROTEIN	CARBS	FATS	FRUITS / VEGGIES	CALORIES

TODAYS WORKOUT

TIME:

EXERCISE	SETS	REPS	WEIGHT	REST	NOTE

DAILY FOOD INTAKE & FITNESS ROUTINE

BREAKFAST

TIME:

DESCRIPTION:

PROTEIN	CARBS	FATS	FRUITS / VEGGIES	CALORIES

SNACK

TIME:

DESCRIPTION:

PROTEIN	CARBS	FATS	FRUITS / VEGGIES	CALORIES

LUNCH

TIME:

DESCRIPTION:

PROTEIN	CARBS	FATS	FRUITS / VEGGIES	CALORIES

SNACK

DESCRIPTION:

PROTEIN	CARBS	FATS	FRUITS / VEGGIES	CALORIES

DINNER

TIME:

DESCRIPTION:

PROTEIN	CARBS	FATS	FRUITS / VEGGIES	CALORIES

TODAYS WORKOUT

TIME:

EXERCISE	SETS	REPS	WEIGHT	REST	NOTE

DAILY FOOD INTAKE & FITNESS ROUTINE

BREAKFAST

TIME:

DESCRIPTION:

PROTEIN	CARBS	FATS	FRUITS / VEGGIES	CALORIES

SNACK

TIME:

DESCRIPTION:

PROTEIN	CARBS	FATS	FRUITS / VEGGIES	CALORIES

LUNCH

TIME:

DESCRIPTION:

PROTEIN	CARBS	FATS	FRUITS / VEGGIES	CALORIES

SNACK

DESCRIPTION:

PROTEIN	CARBS	FATS	FRUITS / VEGGIES	CALORIES

DINNER

TIME:

DESCRIPTION:

PROTEIN	CARBS	FATS	FRUITS / VEGGIES	CALORIES

TODAYS WORKOUT

TIME:

EXERCISE	SETS	REPS	WEIGHT	REST	NOTE

DAILY FOOD INTAKE & FITNESS ROUTINE

BREAKFAST

TIME:

DESCRIPTION:

PROTEIN	CARBS	FATS	FRUITS / VEGGIES	CALORIES

SNACK

TIME:

DESCRIPTION:

PROTEIN	CARBS	FATS	FRUITS / VEGGIES	CALORIES

LUNCH

TIME:

DESCRIPTION:

PROTEIN	CARBS	FATS	FRUITS / VEGGIES	CALORIES

SNACK

DESCRIPTION:
_____
_____
_____

PROTEIN	CARBS	FATS	FRUITS / VEGGIES	CALORIES

DINNER

TIME:

DESCRIPTION:
_____
_____
_____
_____
_____

PROTEIN	CARBS	FATS	FRUITS / VEGGIES	CALORIES

TODAYS WORKOUT

TIME:

EXERCISE	SETS	REPS	WEIGHT	REST	NOTE

DAILY FOOD INTAKE & FITNESS ROUTINE

BREAKFAST
TIME:

DESCRIPTION:

PROTEIN	CARBS	FATS	FRUITS / VEGGIES	CALORIES

SNACK
TIME:

DESCRIPTION:

PROTEIN	CARBS	FATS	FRUITS / VEGGIES	CALORIES

LUNCH
TIME:

DESCRIPTION:

PROTEIN	CARBS	FATS	FRUITS / VEGGIES	CALORIES

SNACK

DESCRIPTION:

PROTEIN	CARBS	FATS	FRUITS / VEGGIES	CALORIES

DINNER

TIME:

DESCRIPTION:

PROTEIN	CARBS	FATS	FRUITS / VEGGIES	CALORIES

TODAYS WORKOUT

TIME:

EXERCISE	SETS	REPS	WEIGHT	REST	NOTE

DAILY FOOD INTAKE & FITNESS ROUTINE

BREAKFAST

TIME:

DESCRIPTION:

PROTEIN	CARBS	FATS	FRUITS / VEGGIES	CALORIES

SNACK

TIME:

DESCRIPTION:

PROTEIN	CARBS	FATS	FRUITS / VEGGIES	CALORIES

LUNCH

TIME:

DESCRIPTION:

PROTEIN	CARBS	FATS	FRUITS / VEGGIES	CALORIES

SNACK

DESCRIPTION:

PROTEIN	CARBS	FATS	FRUITS / VEGGIES	CALORIES

DINNER

TIME:

DESCRIPTION:

PROTEIN	CARBS	FATS	FRUITS / VEGGIES	CALORIES

TODAYS WORKOUT

TIME:

EXERCISE	SETS	REPS	WEIGHT	REST	NOTE

DAILY FOOD INTAKE & FITNESS ROUTINE

BREAKFAST

TIME:

DESCRIPTION:

PROTEIN	CARBS	FATS	FRUITS / VEGGIES	CALORIES

SNACK

TIME:

DESCRIPTION:

PROTEIN	CARBS	FATS	FRUITS / VEGGIES	CALORIES

LUNCH

TIME:

DESCRIPTION:

PROTEIN	CARBS	FATS	FRUITS / VEGGIES	CALORIES

SNACK

DESCRIPTION:

PROTEIN	CARBS	FATS	FRUITS / VEGGIES	CALORIES

DINNER

TIME:

DESCRIPTION:

PROTEIN	CARBS	FATS	FRUITS / VEGGIES	CALORIES

TODAYS WORKOUT

TIME:

EXERCISE	SETS	REPS	WEIGHT	REST	NOTE

DAILY FOOD INTAKE & FITNESS ROUTINE

BREAKFAST

TIME:

DESCRIPTION:

PROTEIN	CARBS	FATS	FRUITS / VEGGIES	CALORIES

SNACK

TIME:

DESCRIPTION:

PROTEIN	CARBS	FATS	FRUITS / VEGGIES	CALORIES

LUNCH

TIME:

DESCRIPTION:

PROTEIN	CARBS	FATS	FRUITS / VEGGIES	CALORIES

SNACK

DESCRIPTION:

PROTEIN	CARBS	FATS	FRUITS / VEGGIES	CALORIES

DINNER

TIME:

DESCRIPTION:

PROTEIN	CARBS	FATS	FRUITS / VEGGIES	CALORIES

TODAYS WORKOUT

TIME:

EXERCISE	SETS	REPS	WEIGHT	REST	NOTE

DAILY FOOD INTAKE & FITNESS ROUTINE

BREAKFAST

TIME:

DESCRIPTION:

PROTEIN	CARBS	FATS	FRUITS / VEGGIES	CALORIES

SNACK

TIME:

DESCRIPTION:

PROTEIN	CARBS	FATS	FRUITS / VEGGIES	CALORIES

LUNCH

TIME:

DESCRIPTION:

PROTEIN	CARBS	FATS	FRUITS / VEGGIES	CALORIES

SNACK

TIME:

DESCRIPTION:

PROTEIN	CARBS	FATS	FRUITS / VEGGIES	CALORIES

DINNER

TIME:

DESCRIPTION:

PROTEIN	CARBS	FATS	FRUITS / VEGGIES	CALORIES

TODAYS WORKOUT

TIME:

EXERCISE	SETS	REPS	WEIGHT	REST	NOTE

DAILY FOOD INTAKE & FITNESS ROUTINE

BREAKFAST

TIME:

DESCRIPTION:

PROTEIN	CARBS	FATS	FRUITS / VEGGIES	CALORIES

SNACK

TIME:

DESCRIPTION:

PROTEIN	CARBS	FATS	FRUITS / VEGGIES	CALORIES

LUNCH

TIME:

DESCRIPTION:

PROTEIN	CARBS	FATS	FRUITS / VEGGIES	CALORIES

SNACK

TIME:

DESCRIPTION:

PROTEIN	CARBS	FATS	FRUITS / VEGGIES	CALORIES

DINNER

TIME:

DESCRIPTION:

PROTEIN	CARBS	FATS	FRUITS / VEGGIES	CALORIES

TODAYS WORKOUT

TIME:

EXERCISE	SETS	REPS	WEIGHT	REST	NOTE

DAILY FOOD INTAKE & FITNESS ROUTINE

BREAKFAST

TIME:

DESCRIPTION:

PROTEIN	CARBS	FATS	FRUITS / VEGGIES	CALORIES

SNACK

TIME:

DESCRIPTION:

PROTEIN	CARBS	FATS	FRUITS / VEGGIES	CALORIES

LUNCH

TIME:

DESCRIPTION:

PROTEIN	CARBS	FATS	FRUITS / VEGGIES	CALORIES

SNACK

DESCRIPTION:

PROTEIN	CARBS	FATS	FRUITS / VEGGIES	CALORIES

DINNER

TIME:

DESCRIPTION:

PROTEIN	CARBS	FATS	FRUITS / VEGGIES	CALORIES

TODAYS WORKOUT

TIME:

EXERCISE	SETS	REPS	WEIGHT	REST	NOTE

DAILY FOOD INTAKE & FITNESS ROUTINE

BREAKFAST

TIME:

DESCRIPTION:

PROTEIN	CARBS	FATS	FRUITS / VEGGIES	CALORIES

SNACK

TIME:

DESCRIPTION:

PROTEIN	CARBS	FATS	FRUITS / VEGGIES	CALORIES

LUNCH

TIME:

DESCRIPTION:

PROTEIN	CARBS	FATS	FRUITS / VEGGIES	CALORIES

SNACK

TIME:

DESCRIPTION:

PROTEIN	CARBS	FATS	FRUITS / VEGGIES	CALORIES

DINNER

TIME:

DESCRIPTION:

PROTEIN	CARBS	FATS	FRUITS / VEGGIES	CALORIES

TODAYS WORKOUT

TIME:

EXERCISE	SETS	REPS	WEIGHT	REST	NOTE

DAILY FOOD INTAKE & FITNESS ROUTINE

BREAKFAST

TIME:

DESCRIPTION:

PROTEIN	CARBS	FATS	FRUITS / VEGGIES	CALORIES

SNACK

TIME:

DESCRIPTION:

PROTEIN	CARBS	FATS	FRUITS / VEGGIES	CALORIES

LUNCH

TIME:

DESCRIPTION:

PROTEIN	CARBS	FATS	FRUITS / VEGGIES	CALORIES

SNACK

DESCRIPTION:

PROTEIN	CARBS	FATS	FRUITS / VEGGIES	CALORIES

DINNER

TIME:

DESCRIPTION:

PROTEIN	CARBS	FATS	FRUITS / VEGGIES	CALORIES

TODAYS WORKOUT

TIME:

EXERCISE	SETS	REPS	WEIGHT	REST	NOTE

DAILY FOOD INTAKE & FITNESS ROUTINE

BREAKFAST

TIME:

DESCRIPTION:

PROTEIN	CARBS	FATS	FRUITS / VEGGIES	CALORIES

SNACK

TIME:

DESCRIPTION:

PROTEIN	CARBS	FATS	FRUITS / VEGGIES	CALORIES

LUNCH

TIME:

DESCRIPTION:

PROTEIN	CARBS	FATS	FRUITS / VEGGIES	CALORIES

SNACK

DESCRIPTION:

PROTEIN	CARBS	FATS	FRUITS / VEGGIES	CALORIES

DINNER

TIME:

DESCRIPTION:

PROTEIN	CARBS	FATS	FRUITS / VEGGIES	CALORIES

TODAYS WORKOUT

TIME:

EXERCISE	SETS	REPS	WEIGHT	REST	NOTE

DAILY FOOD INTAKE & FITNESS ROUTINE

BREAKFAST

TIME:

DESCRIPTION:

PROTEIN	CARBS	FATS	FRUITS / VEGGIES	CALORIES

SNACK

TIME:

DESCRIPTION:

PROTEIN	CARBS	FATS	FRUITS / VEGGIES	CALORIES

LUNCH

TIME:

DESCRIPTION:

PROTEIN	CARBS	FATS	FRUITS / VEGGIES	CALORIES

SNACK

DESCRIPTION:

PROTEIN	CARBS	FATS	FRUITS / VEGGIES	CALORIES

DINNER

TIME:

DESCRIPTION:

PROTEIN	CARBS	FATS	FRUITS / VEGGIES	CALORIES

TODAYS WORKOUT

TIME:

EXERCISE	SETS	REPS	WEIGHT	REST	NOTE

DAILY FOOD INTAKE & FITNESS ROUTINE

BREAKFAST

TIME:

DESCRIPTION:

PROTEIN	CARBS	FATS	FRUITS / VEGGIES	CALORIES

SNACK

TIME:

DESCRIPTION:

PROTEIN	CARBS	FATS	FRUITS / VEGGIES	CALORIES

LUNCH

TIME:

DESCRIPTION:

PROTEIN	CARBS	FATS	FRUITS / VEGGIES	CALORIES

SNACK

DESCRIPTION:

PROTEIN	CARBS	FATS	FRUITS / VEGGIES	CALORIES

DINNER

TIME:

DESCRIPTION:

PROTEIN	CARBS	FATS	FRUITS / VEGGIES	CALORIES

TODAYS WORKOUT

TIME:

EXERCISE	SETS	REPS	WEIGHT	REST	NOTE

DAILY FOOD INTAKE & FITNESS ROUTINE

BREAKFAST

TIME:

DESCRIPTION:

PROTEIN	CARBS	FATS	FRUITS / VEGGIES	CALORIES

SNACK

TIME:

DESCRIPTION:

PROTEIN	CARBS	FATS	FRUITS / VEGGIES	CALORIES

LUNCH

TIME:

DESCRIPTION:

PROTEIN	CARBS	FATS	FRUITS / VEGGIES	CALORIES

SNACK

TIME:

DESCRIPTION:

PROTEIN	CARBS	FATS	FRUITS / VEGGIES	CALORIES

DINNER

TIME:

DESCRIPTION:

PROTEIN	CARBS	FATS	FRUITS / VEGGIES	CALORIES

TODAYS WORKOUT

TIME:

EXERCISE	SETS	REPS	WEIGHT	REST	NOTE

DAILY FOOD INTAKE & FITNESS ROUTINE

BREAKFAST

TIME:

DESCRIPTION:

PROTEIN	CARBS	FATS	FRUITS / VEGGIES	CALORIES

SNACK

TIME:

DESCRIPTION:

PROTEIN	CARBS	FATS	FRUITS / VEGGIES	CALORIES

LUNCH

TIME:

DESCRIPTION:

PROTEIN	CARBS	FATS	FRUITS / VEGGIES	CALORIES

SNACK

DESCRIPTION:

PROTEIN	CARBS	FATS	FRUITS / VEGGIES	CALORIES

DINNER

TIME:

DESCRIPTION:

PROTEIN	CARBS	FATS	FRUITS / VEGGIES	CALORIES

TODAYS WORKOUT

TIME:

EXERCISE	SETS	REPS	WEIGHT	REST	NOTE

DAILY FOOD INTAKE & FITNESS ROUTINE

BREAKFAST

TIME:

DESCRIPTION:

PROTEIN	CARBS	FATS	FRUITS / VEGGIES	CALORIES

SNACK

TIME:

DESCRIPTION:

PROTEIN	CARBS	FATS	FRUITS / VEGGIES	CALORIES

LUNCH

TIME:

DESCRIPTION:

PROTEIN	CARBS	FATS	FRUITS / VEGGIES	CALORIES

SNACK

TIME:

DESCRIPTION:

PROTEIN	CARBS	FATS	FRUITS / VEGGIES	CALORIES

DINNER

TIME:

DESCRIPTION:

PROTEIN	CARBS	FATS	FRUITS / VEGGIES	CALORIES

TODAYS WORKOUT

TIME:

EXERCISE	SETS	REPS	WEIGHT	REST	NOTE

DAILY FOOD INTAKE & FITNESS ROUTINE

BREAKFAST

TIME:

DESCRIPTION:

PROTEIN	CARBS	FATS	FRUITS / VEGGIES	CALORIES

SNACK

TIME:

DESCRIPTION:

PROTEIN	CARBS	FATS	FRUITS / VEGGIES	CALORIES

LUNCH

TIME:

DESCRIPTION:

PROTEIN	CARBS	FATS	FRUITS / VEGGIES	CALORIES

SNACK

DESCRIPTION:

PROTEIN	CARBS	FATS	FRUITS / VEGGIES	CALORIES

DINNER

TIME:

DESCRIPTION:

PROTEIN	CARBS	FATS	FRUITS / VEGGIES	CALORIES

TODAYS WORKOUT

TIME:

EXERCISE	SETS	REPS	WEIGHT	REST	NOTE

DAILY FOOD INTAKE & FITNESS ROUTINE

BREAKFAST

TIME:

DESCRIPTION:

PROTEIN	CARBS	FATS	FRUITS / VEGGIES	CALORIES

SNACK

TIME:

DESCRIPTION:

PROTEIN	CARBS	FATS	FRUITS / VEGGIES	CALORIES

LUNCH

TIME:

DESCRIPTION:

PROTEIN	CARBS	FATS	FRUITS / VEGGIES	CALORIES

SNACK

DESCRIPTION:

PROTEIN	CARBS	FATS	FRUITS / VEGGIES	CALORIES

DINNER

TIME:

DESCRIPTION:

PROTEIN	CARBS	FATS	FRUITS / VEGGIES	CALORIES

TODAYS WORKOUT

TIME:

EXERCISE	SETS	REPS	WEIGHT	REST	NOTE

DAILY FOOD INTAKE & FITNESS ROUTINE

BREAKFAST
TIME:

DESCRIPTION:

PROTEIN	CARBS	FATS	FRUITS / VEGGIES	CALORIES

SNACK
TIME:

DESCRIPTION:

PROTEIN	CARBS	FATS	FRUITS / VEGGIES	CALORIES

LUNCH
TIME:

DESCRIPTION:

PROTEIN	CARBS	FATS	FRUITS / VEGGIES	CALORIES

SNACK

DESCRIPTION:

PROTEIN	CARBS	FATS	FRUITS / VEGGIES	CALORIES

DINNER

TIME:

DESCRIPTION:

PROTEIN	CARBS	FATS	FRUITS / VEGGIES	CALORIES

TODAYS WORKOUT

TIME:

EXERCISE	SETS	REPS	WEIGHT	REST	NOTE

DAILY FOOD INTAKE & FITNESS ROUTINE

BREAKFAST

TIME:

DESCRIPTION:

PROTEIN	CARBS	FATS	FRUITS / VEGGIES	CALORIES

SNACK

TIME:

DESCRIPTION:

PROTEIN	CARBS	FATS	FRUITS / VEGGIES	CALORIES

LUNCH

TIME:

DESCRIPTION:

PROTEIN	CARBS	FATS	FRUITS / VEGGIES	CALORIES

SNACK

DESCRIPTION:

PROTEIN	CARBS	FATS	FRUITS / VEGGIES	CALORIES

DINNER

TIME:

DESCRIPTION:

PROTEIN	CARBS	FATS	FRUITS / VEGGIES	CALORIES

TODAYS WORKOUT

TIME:

EXERCISE	SETS	REPS	WEIGHT	REST	NOTE

DAILY FOOD INTAKE & FITNESS ROUTINE

BREAKFAST

TIME:

DESCRIPTION:

PROTEIN	CARBS	FATS	FRUITS / VEGGIES	CALORIES

SNACK

TIME:

DESCRIPTION:

PROTEIN	CARBS	FATS	FRUITS / VEGGIES	CALORIES

LUNCH

TIME:

DESCRIPTION:

PROTEIN	CARBS	FATS	FRUITS / VEGGIES	CALORIES

SNACK

DESCRIPTION:

PROTEIN	CARBS	FATS	FRUITS / VEGGIES	CALORIES

DINNER

TIME:

DESCRIPTION:

PROTEIN	CARBS	FATS	FRUITS / VEGGIES	CALORIES

TODAYS WORKOUT

TIME:

EXERCISE	SETS	REPS	WEIGHT	REST	NOTE

DAILY FOOD INTAKE & FITNESS ROUTINE

BREAKFAST
TIME:

DESCRIPTION:

PROTEIN	CARBS	FATS	FRUITS / VEGGIES	CALORIES

SNACK
TIME:

DESCRIPTION:

PROTEIN	CARBS	FATS	FRUITS / VEGGIES	CALORIES

LUNCH
TIME:

DESCRIPTION:

PROTEIN	CARBS	FATS	FRUITS / VEGGIES	CALORIES

SNACK

DESCRIPTION:

PROTEIN	CARBS	FATS	FRUITS / VEGGIES	CALORIES

DINNER

TIME:

DESCRIPTION:

PROTEIN	CARBS	FATS	FRUITS / VEGGIES	CALORIES

TODAYS WORKOUT

TIME:

EXERCISE	SETS	REPS	WEIGHT	REST	NOTE

DAILY FOOD INTAKE & FITNESS ROUTINE

BREAKFAST

TIME:

DESCRIPTION:

PROTEIN	CARBS	FATS	FRUITS / VEGGIES	CALORIES

SNACK

TIME:

DESCRIPTION:

PROTEIN	CARBS	FATS	FRUITS / VEGGIES	CALORIES

LUNCH

TIME:

DESCRIPTION:

PROTEIN	CARBS	FATS	FRUITS / VEGGIES	CALORIES

SNACK

DESCRIPTION:

PROTEIN	CARBS	FATS	FRUITS / VEGGIES	CALORIES

DINNER

TIME:

DESCRIPTION:

PROTEIN	CARBS	FATS	FRUITS / VEGGIES	CALORIES

TODAYS WORKOUT

TIME:

EXERCISE	SETS	REPS	WEIGHT	REST	NOTE

DAILY FOOD INTAKE & FITNESS ROUTINE

BREAKFAST

TIME:

DESCRIPTION:

PROTEIN	CARBS	FATS	FRUITS / VEGGIES	CALORIES

SNACK

TIME:

DESCRIPTION:

PROTEIN	CARBS	FATS	FRUITS / VEGGIES	CALORIES

LUNCH

TIME:

DESCRIPTION:

PROTEIN	CARBS	FATS	FRUITS / VEGGIES	CALORIES

SNACK

DESCRIPTION:

PROTEIN	CARBS	FATS	FRUITS / VEGGIES	CALORIES

DINNER

TIME:

DESCRIPTION:

PROTEIN	CARBS	FATS	FRUITS / VEGGIES	CALORIES

TODAYS WORKOUT

TIME:

EXERCISE	SETS	REPS	WEIGHT	REST	NOTE

www.ingramcontent.com/pod-product-compliance
Lightning Source LLC
Chambersburg PA
CBHW080721290626
47170CB00017B/2870